FAMOUS LIVES

Louis Pasteur

by Karen Wallace

Illustrations by Lesley Bisseker

First published in 1997
by Franklin Watts
This edition 2002

Franklin Watts
96 Leonard Street
London EC2A 4XD

Franklin Watts Australia
56 O'Riordan Street
Alexandria, Sydney
NSW 2015

ISBN 0 7496 4338 2 (pbk)

A CIP catalogue record for this book is
available from the British Library

Dewey Decimal Classification
Number: 616.009

Series Editor: Sarah Ridley
Designer: Kirstie Billingham
Consultant: Dr. Anne Millard

Printed in Great Britain

Louis Pasteur

Louis Pasteur was born in a small village in France in 1822. His father was a leather-worker but he wanted his son, Louis, to be a teacher. As it turned out, Louis became one of the greatest scientists of his century!

At first Louis was only an average pupil. He liked painting and painted many pictures of his friends and family.

It was his school teacher who first noticed that Louis was much cleverer than he appeared.

Louis was sent away to school in Paris but he was very homesick and only stayed a few weeks.

A few years later he returned to Paris and was taught by a famous chemist called Professor Dumas.

At the end of his first year Louis won many prizes. Soon he became a professor and was awarded a gold medal for his work on crystals.

Congratulations! You have achieved great things already.

Watch this space!

In 1849, Louis Pasteur married
Marie Laurent. Marie was a kind
patient woman who understood
her husband's dedication to
his research.

Louis studied long into the night and often on Sundays as well.

Louis filled many notebooks with his experiments. He believed that great discoveries didn't happen by chance alone. Hard work was just as important.

Around this time, the French wine industry was in terrible trouble. Their wine was going sour and they didn't know why.

They lost lots of money and men were frightened of losing their jobs, as well. They turned to Louis for help.

11

After many experiments, Louis discovered that the problem was caused by some of the yeasts used in making wine.
The solution was simple: heat the wine just enough to kill off the harmful yeasts.

The wine makers were horrified.

You can't heat wine!

It will ruin the flavour!

Nobody will drink it!

But they were wrong. Soon other liquids, like milk and beer, were heated in the same way. This made them safe to drink. The process was called

This milk tastes great, but will it make us feel sick?

pasteurization after Louis Pasteur. Up until then, many children and adults became ill drinking milk that contained germs.

In 1857, when he was only thirty-five, Louis was appointed Director at a very important school in Paris. But there were no laboratories and no equipment for him to carry on his research.

So Louis set up his own
laboratory in two attic rooms.
They were so small he had to
crawl in on his hands and knees.

At this time, France was plagued by diseases like cholera and typhoid.

Scientists still didn't understand how these diseases spread. Many believed that tiny disease-carrying particles just appeared on their own.

Pasteur knew that the particles that carry diseases had to come from *something* and from *somewhere*. He had recently lost his eldest daughter to typhoid fever.

Perhaps this was one of the reasons he was so determined to find out the truth.

His experiment was simple.
He filled a number of flasks with
different liquids. He heated them
all to kill off the germs. Then he
sealed half of them and left the
other half open.

These ones smell nasty and diseased!

When Pasteur observed the
difference between the liquids in
the flasks, he made two of the
most important discoveries of
his century.

24

1/ Tiny germs live in the air.

2/ Diseases are caused by tiny germs.

By now Pasteur's reputation had spread all over Europe. In 1867 he won the Grand Prize Medal for saving the French wine industry.

At the same time, a mysterious disease was attacking silkworms threatening the silk industry.

After much research Pasteur discovered the problem: a tiny worm was infecting the leaves.

Shortly afterwards, at the age of forty-five, all the hard work took its toll. Pasteur collapsed and suffered a stroke.

But even though he was paralysed in his left arm and left leg for the rest of his life, he carried on with his research.

Pasteur had discovered that disease was carried by germs in the air. Now he wanted to find a way to stop disease spreading.

At that time a terrible sickness called anthrax killed thousands of sheep and cattle every year all over Europe.

Pasteur discovered that the anthrax germ could survive in the earth inside earthworms for many years.

At first he advised farmers just as he had advised the silkworm producers. They must burn all their sick animals and abandon the infected fields.

Then Pasteur came up with another idea. He noticed that an animal who caught anthrax and survived, never caught anthrax again.

He decided to inject a flock of sheep with a weak solution of anthrax germs.

Then he put them out to graze
with other sheep on a field
infected with anthrax.

The injected flock lived.
All the other sheep died.
Pasteur had found a vaccination
against anthrax!

Immediately scientists made a vaccination to stop chicken cholera and swine fever.

By now Pasteur was getting old and his health was failing. But the greatest challenge was still to come!

Rabies was a horrible disease that killed animals and humans. Pasteur decided to make a vaccination from infected rabbits and test it on dogs.

The big question was:
Would it work on humans?

One morning a little boy called Joseph Meister arrived at Pasteur's laboratory. He had been bitten by a rabid dog. Pasteur's animal vaccination was the little boy's only chance.

Pasteur was in a dilemma.

41

Joseph was injected with Pasteur's vaccine and he survived!

Immediately the news flashed
around the world.

A special school was started in Paris. It was called the Pasteur Institute. Money poured in from everywhere to help build it.

Louis Pasteur died in 1895 but the Institute set up in his honour lives on. Like its founder, it works to understand and prevent disease all over the world.

PASTEUR INSTITUTE

founded 1888

Diptheria ✓

Plague ✓

Further facts

Hospitals

Conditions in
hospitals in
the nineteenth
century were
terrible. Nobody

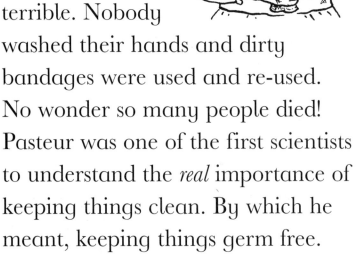

washed their hands and dirty
bandages were used and re-used.
No wonder so many people died!
Pasteur was one of the first scientists
to understand the *real* importance of
keeping things clean. By which he
meant, keeping things germ free.

Pasteur himself was so obsessed by
germs he even thought the custom of
shaking hands was rather unhealthy!

Pasteur's tomb

Pasteur was buried with huge ceremony. The walls of the crypt around his tomb are painted with children, dogs, lambs and chickens and others whose lives he helped to save.

Diseases and germs

A germ is another word for the tiny organism that causes disease. It was

Anthrax

Pasteur's greatest achievement that he proved that diseases don't just happen. They are caused by particular germs.

Some important dates in Louis Pasteur's lifetime

1822   Louis Pasteur was born on December 22.

1843-48 Louis studies chemistry in Paris with Professor Dumas.

1849   Louis marries Marie Laurent.

1857-65 Louis studies yeasts and solves the wine industry's problem.

1867   Louis wins a gold medal for saving the French wine industry.

1868   Louis suffers his first stroke.

1870   Louis studies a silkworm disease and solves the silkworm problem.

1882   Louis discovers the vaccine for anthrax.

1885   Louis saves Joseph Meister from rabies

1888   Louis becomes Director of the Pasteur Institute.

1895   Louis dies on September 8.